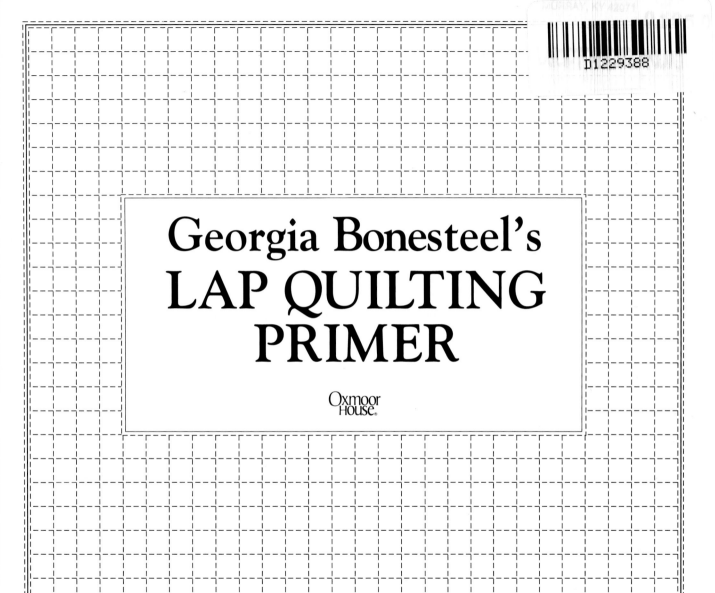

Georgia Bonesteel's
LAP QUILTING PRIMER

Oxmoor
House®

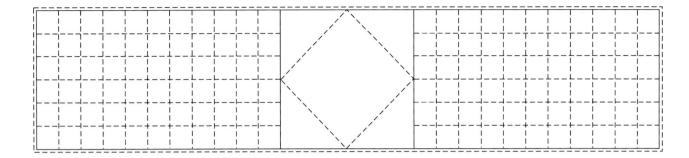

CONTENTS

©1991 by Oxmoor House, Inc.
Book Division of Southern Progress Corporation
P.O. Box 2463, Birmingham, AL 35201

ISBN: 0-8487-0892-X
Manufactured in the United States of America
First Printing 1991

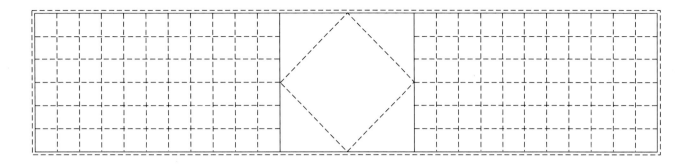

STARTING FROM SCRATCH

DEFINITION

Lap quilting is the technique of joining 3 layers—a decorative top, batting, and backing—together in block-sized sections. The blocks are quilted individually and then sewn together to build an entire quilt. Lap quilting is sometimes called sectional quilting, quilt-as-you-go, apartment quilting, or the portable quilt. Nowadays, few of us have room for a big quilting frame, and many of us work outside the home. This leaves us with limited craft time. Working in smaller sections, quilting "as you go," has obvious appeal.

Some designs, however, call for a large pieced center section or center panel, and these can be quilted using a portable hoop. Whether you are quilting individual blocks or interior panels, each step in the lap-quilting process has its rewards and is dependent on the other steps for its success.

LAP QUILTING TERMINOLOGY

Being proud of and secure in your work starts with an understanding of definitions. Let's take a look at some basic quilting and sewing terminology.

Appliqué: Cutout figures sewn to a larger foundation piece of fabric. This application can be made in several ways: basting raw edges under and then securing with a hidden slipstitch; buttonhole-stitching on top of raw edges; or working raw edges under ⅛", clipping curves as you go, and attaching with a slipstitch. A close-set, machine zigzag stitch (satin stitch) over raw edges may also be used.

Backing: The bottom or back layer of a quilt; the underneath side. Muslin is often used because it highlights the quilting stitches, and it is inexpensive. Dark-colored backings are not the best choice for a beginner using white quilting thread, because the stitches are prominent. Print fabrics tend to

hide the stitches completely. In lap quilting, a design can be created on the back of the quilt by alternating the position of the pattern of the fabric. (Be careful when trying to match large checks or prints. Sometimes the horizontal and vertical design of the pattern may not run true, and it may not be possible to match them.)

Backstitch: A handstitch made by inserting the point of the needle behind the thread each time and coming up ahead of it. It is used in hand piecing to strengthen a running stitch and in quilting to end off. When quilting and almost out of thread, loop the thread and form a knot close to the fabric. Then backstitch into the quilt top and pull the thread through the batting.

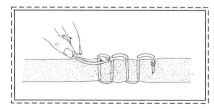

Backstitch for Quilting Diagram.

Come back up about an inch away from stitching; clip off. (See Backstitch for Quilting Diagram.)

Basting: A temporary running stitch used to secure fabrics prior to machine stitching or hand quilting. It is best done with a contrasting thread that is easy to see. Some black cotton threads leave a tiny black spot upon removal, so test your basting thread. Basting is a very important feature of lap quilting because it holds the 3 layers together for quilting.

Batting: The filler or middle part of the quilt "sandwich"—the insulation. Today, polyester batting is most widely used and is available in various weights and thicknesses. No matter what type of batting you prefer to use, make sure that it has been bonded.

Block: A unit of patchwork, usually in the shape of a square, repeated to construct an entire quilt top. Blocks may be attached directly to each other (block-to-block assembly) or may be separated by borders.

Basic Patchwork Block Classifications:

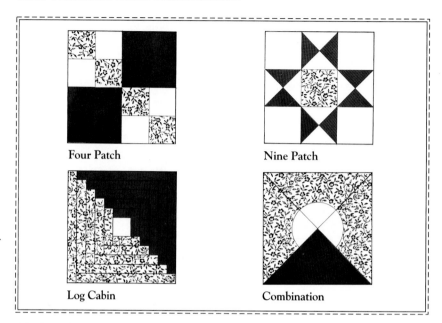

Four Patch

Nine Patch

Log Cabin

Combination

Block-to-block assembly: In lap quilting, the process of joining quilted blocks to form horizontal or vertical rows.

Borders: Narrow panels that set off each block in a quilt. (Borders around blocks are sometimes referred to as sashing.) The corners of borders may be mitered or squared off with small squares in a contrasting color. Borders may have appliqué accents or may be pieced to create a new design. Borders may also be added to the perimeter of a quilt that needs more length or width.

"Cattywampus": A quilter's term for an uneven angle of cloth resulting from a lack of basting or an unsuccessful quilt connection.

Chatelaine: A scissor forget-me-not to be worn around the neck when quilting or doing any needlework. It enables you to "keep it together"—needles, thread, thimble, and pins.

Connection: The joining of 3 layers—block, batting, backing—for quilting. In assembly, sewing sections together to form the lap-quilting connection.

Cross-hatching: A quilting design formed by parallel lines that intersect.

Crazy patch: A form of patchwork in which odd shapes of fabric are machine-stitched to a foundation block. Embroidery stitches are then applied to accent the seams. String quilts also fall into this category.

Dangling thread: A loose, unknotted thread left in a quilted area to be rethreaded in order to complete quilting after the quilt is assembled.

Dog-ears: The triangular extensions formed at the points where diagonal pieces are sewn together. Clipping them relieves the block of excess bulk.

Edging or Binding: Strips of fabric such as bias tape, used to enclose the perimeter of a quilt.

"Eyeball": To estimate a dimension by looking it over, rather than using a measuring device.

Flexicurve: A flexible drafting tool that enables the quilter and seamstress to draw and create smooth curves; it may also be used as a guide for marking curved lines for quilting. The ½"-wide base accommodates ¼" seams.

Fudge: An irresistible chocolate candy, but in sewing, it means to hedge or cheat a little when joining fabric!

Grain line: The direction of the weave or construction of the yarns in fabric. Warp yarns are the lengthwise axis of the fabric and run parallel to the selvage, while the weft yarns run crosswise. Any line on the fabric that is not parallel to either the warp or the weft yarns is considered to be off-grain.

Marking: The process of transferring designs onto the quilt top in order to have a line to follow when quilting. Marking implements include fabric marker, water-soluble pen, thin slivers of soap, pencils(test your fabric first for easy removal), adhesive-backed paper cut in special shapes, and masking tape. The goal is for the quilting to dominate and the marking line to disappear.

Mitering: The creation of a diagonal seam at the meeting of 2 borders to form a right angle.

Off hand: The hand that rests under the quilt, guiding the needle and checking that all 3 layers have been caught by it. The finger that feels the point of the needle repeatedly should be protected with a thimble, masking tape, a coat of clear nail polish, or the fingertip from an old leather glove.

Patchwork: The art of building a large piece of decorative cloth from smaller pieces.

Piecing or piecework: The process of sewing 2 or more pieces of fabric together to form a design. Piecing can be done by hand or on the sewing machine with a regular-length stitch, coordinating thread, and a ¼" seam allowance.

Quilt: A bed cover with 3 layers; a "sandwich" comprised of the decorative top, the filler or batting, and the bottom layer or backing. These layers are secured with running stitches (quilting) or with yarn knots (tufting).

Row-to-row assembly: In lap quilting, the process of setting together rows of quilted blocks to form a quilt.

Setting: The relationship or arrangement of blocks that form the quilt top.

Stencil: A template used for transferring a quilting design to the quilt top to provide a guide for quilting stitches.

Template: A pattern made from durable material (cardboard, plastic, sandpaper, or soft, transparent vinyl) for patchwork shapes. Templates are a key factor in precision piecework, ensuring uniformity in size and shape.

Trapunto: A softly sculptured effect, created by stuffing a design on a quilt from the back or underside, giving the design more dimension.

QUILTING NECESSITIES

Two necessities not available at the notions counter are a strong desire to make a quilt and the patience to stick with it when piecework goes askew. Other quilting necessities are listed below.

This list may appear overwhelming at first, but you will not need to purchase every item immediately. Check your sewing basket; you may find that you already have many of the following items on hand. As your quilting develops, so will your inventory of tools and notions. Drafting equipment stores sell a wonder of instruments that can be used for precise marking and pattern making.

Remember, the perfect straight line, the precise cut, and the exact angle all combine to create your ultimate goal—the warm and beautiful quilt.

Batting: Polyester and perfected cotton comes in rolled sheets that are unrolled and cut in sections in preparation for quilting. Batting can be pieced in the middle because it will be secured by your quilting stitches.

Bias bars and bias tape makers: Bias bars assist you in making the narrowest of folded bias strips, especially useful for appliquéd designs. Bias tape makers fold bias strips automatically into various widths to use as edging or binding for your quilt.

Drawing implements: A compass, drafting triangle, and a selection of rulers are the basic set of implements you will need. Clear plastic rulers, thick and thin, with ¼" marking on the straight edges are invaluable. There are many types of rulers on the market; to start with, a 6" square and a 6" x 24" ruler will fit your needs.

Embroidery floss: Three strands of floss are used for appliqué and crazy patchwork.

Fold-out cutting board for fabric: A gridded board assures perfect alignment of fabric when marking and cutting pieces.

Graph paper: Graph paper is used to draw quilt blocks and the whole quilt. This step can help you with color selection and calculation of fabric yardages.

Grid-grip: Grid-grip is a polycoated paper with a continuous grid that is used as a design and template tool.

Hole punch: A handheld hole punch that cuts a ⅛" diameter circle aids in making accurate templates.

Hoops: Hoops are used to hold fabric for quilting. These are optional in lap quilting, depending on your expertise in handling the basted, layered material. They come in round, oval, and square shapes, as well as a supported form that rests on your lap or a table.

Iron: A steam iron and ironing board are essential to the piecework process.

Marking devices: Pencil, fabric marker, tailors' chalk, or slivers of worn soap can be used to mark quilting designs on the fabric. Be sure to test all marking implements on scraps of fabrics to be sure that the mark can be easily removed.

Masking tape: Any width of masking tape can be used on fabric as a guide for quilting. Placing masking tape on the machine throat plate aids in maintaining an even ¼" seam allowance.

Needles: "Quilting Betweens," sizes 7, 8, 9, 10, 11, and even 12, with large eyes are best. Use embroidery or sewing needles for basting.

Paper, tracing: Tracing paper is used to duplicate patterns and quilting designs.

Permanent marker: Labeling your templates with a marker organizes the quiltmaking process.

Pins: Large, white, round-head pins work well because they slip through fabric easily and are easy to find on deep carpet.

Pincushion: A magnetic pin holder attracts pins and needles and keeps them in one place.

Point turner: This little tool is especially useful when making pillows, vests, and other items where crisp, encased corners are needed.

Quilter's quarter and Lotus circle: The quilter's quarter is a plexiglass rod that is ¼" thick and at least 8" in length. It is used to draw ¼" seam allowances.

The Lotus circle is also used by quilters to mark seam lines. It is a coin-shaped, metal implement, ½" in diameter with a hole in the center. When a pencil point is inserted in the center hole, a ¼" seam allowance can be drawn by moving the Lotus circle around the edges of any template. It is especially useful for curved pieces.

Rotary cutter and mat: A rotary cutter makes cutting layers of straight strips of fabric easy and quick. A gridded mat maintains blade life and ensures precision cutting.

Scissors: Good heavy scissors for cutting layers of fabric (have some sort of identifying mark on these to guard against workshop bandits!) are an absolute necessity. Following is a list of scissors to keep at hand:

- Lightweight scissors for frequent cutting
- Paper scissors for cutting templates
- Embroidery scissors for buttonholes and precision cutting in other tight areas
- Appliqué trimmers
- Thread clippers

Template materials: Patterns made from plain and gridded translucent vinyl can be used repeatedly without wearing down the edges.

Thimbles: One is needed for the middle finger of the hand that guides the needle when quilting, and another is needed to protect the underneath finger on the off hand.

Thread for quilting: Cotton or polyester-wrapped quilting thread with wax coating is recommended for quilting. Additional beeswax may be applied as each thread length is cut.

Thread for sewing machine: Mercerized, cotton-covered, polyester, all-purpose thread is recommended for piecing. Neutral colors such as gray, beige, and taupe blend with many fabric colors. ◆

GETTING UNDER WAY

SELECTING FABRICS

Before the first stitch on your quilt can be taken you must decide on your design and fabric. Since you will live with your choice of color for a long time, think it through carefully. Even if the same fabric and design are chosen by many quilters, each quilt will become one of a kind, for the hands of every quilter apply their own unique touch. Visit libraries and museums, glance through magazines and books to increase your knowledge of quilts and quilt design. Make notes on your favorite colors and patterns and those that leave you cold. Then decide.

Before buying any fabrics, check your supply at home for inspiration and usability. I have found that 100% cotton fabric responds best to small piecework, but I do not rule out using blends. If a fabric's composition is unknown, you might try the burn test to determine if polyester is present. (A "burn test" means just what it says. Burn a small scrap of the fabric. Cotton has a slow, even burn and leaves a fine ash; cotton/polyester burns quickly and gives off black smoke, leaving a dark crust.) Keep velvets, corduroy, and nap fabrics for novelty projects. Eliminate sheer fabrics. Save knit fabrics for another project where raw edges can be overlapped and either hand-stitched or machine-zigzagged in place; their bulk, thickness, and stretching qualities will not adapt to small piecework.

When you purchase fabric, always buy extra to allow for mistakes or a change of mind. The design that looks fine on paper may need altering once piecing is started. Remember, if instead of piecing the border, you are making a border out of a solid piece of fabric, you will need to purchase fabric the length of your quilt. Large fabric remnants left over from cutting the pieces for the quilt blocks can be used for pieced borders.

Before you get started, preshrink purchased fabrics and fabrics on hand. Machine-wash them in warm water, using the normal cycle and a small amount of soap. Then partially dry and steam-press them. (There will be strings, of course.) This procedure ensures a washable quilt and also softens the fabric for the needle. Once preshinking has been completed, eliminate any fabric that fades or bleeds (keep an eye on reds and blacks).

QUILT DESIGN AND SETTINGS

A sampler quilt can be the perfect choice for your first quilt. Each block represents a different story encased in a separate, mitered border (sashing) with its own color scheme. Your inaugural quilt will be a true sampling of bygone blocks—a genuine tribute to traditional quilting. By using leftovers, your quilt becomes a memory quilt composed of sentimental, favorite fabrics. A colorful sampler has another feature— it will fit into any color scheme with a folksy, old-time look.

You may, on the other hand, want to achieve a specific color scheme in a quilt with the sampler concept. In this case, choose 4 co-ordinated fabrics—a print and a geometric design, such as a small check, stripe, or polka dot; and 2 solid colors to blend with them. Choose 20 of your favorite blocks and go to it. You'll have the experience of learning how a number of different blocks are set together, but the result will be one color story. I call this a "sampler theme quilt."

Or you may decide on 10 different blocks alternated either with 1 specific block or with a stenciled design on a solid square. Or a medallion effect can be achieved by highlighting 4 blocks in the center and bordering them with contrasting blocks. You are limited only by your imagination.

If you would like to try your hand at designing new patterns, try cutting pieces out of various colors of construction paper and playing with them as you would with the pieces of a jigsaw puzzle until you find an arrangement that strikes your fancy.

Borders can also change the outcome of a quilt. Consider a small-checked border (do not choose a large check since checked material is woven with a distinct difference in crosswise and lengthwise grain), a print border, an eyelet border, or alternating colors on each border.

There are a variety of quilt edgings (bindings) to use—from a simple bias binding to prairie points. Chapter 6, "The Finishing Touch," provides a brief discussion with illustrations of several of these alternatives.

Obviously, it is important to plan ahead. Drafting your borders and setting on graph paper helps you to visualize the possibilities.

Settings with Mitered Borders (Sashing)

Mitered borders (sashing) and their variations can bring a great deal of originality to the look of your finished quilt. Mitered borders create a frame for your block design. (See Quilt Settings with Mitered Borders—Diagram I.)

Varying the typical mitered border by using two light and two dark borders on opposite sides creates a spinning effect. (See Quilt Settings with Mitered Borders—Diagram II.)

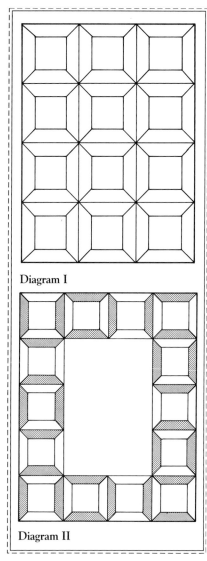

Diagram I

Diagram II

Quilt Settings with Mitered Borders

Inserting a 1"-wide dark accent strip before attaching a mitered border accentuates each of the blocks surrounding the center panel. (See Quilt Settings with Mitered Borders—Diagram III.)

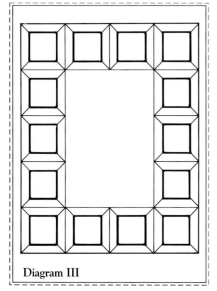

Diagram III

Quilt Settings with Mitered Borders

The Diagonal Setting

Many quilt patterns take on an entirely new look when the blocks are set in diagonal rows. (See Diagonal Quilt Setting Diagram.) Half-blocks (triangles) form the perimeter of a diagonally assembled quilt. A diagonal setting is not suitable, of course, for blocks with a distinct up-and-down pattern.

After all of your blocks are pieced, lay them out row by row. Machine-stitch the triangular half-blocks to the sides of the blocks they border before lap-quilting each block individually. The backing for each of the end blocks—those to which the triangles have been sewn—should be cut so that the diagonal line is on the straight of the grain rather than on the bias.

Diagonal Quilt Setting Diagram

Square Insets

A favorite old-fashioned way of setting a quilt involves the use of square insets between the corners of blocks. While single squares and small four-patch insets are most commonly used (see Quilt Settings with Single and Four-Patch

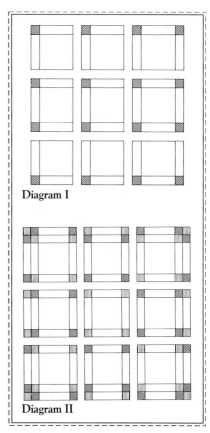

Diagram I

Diagram II

Quilt Settings with Single and Four-Patch Insets

Insets—Diagrams I and II), even nine-patch insets are possible. (See Quilt Setting with Nine-Patch Insets Diagram.)

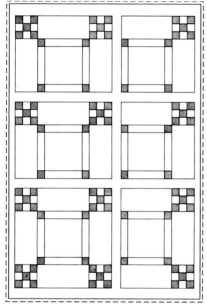

Quilt Setting with Nine-Patch Insets

Because these insets are shared by blocks, individual blocks are pieced and quilted with differing numbers of borders. When the blocks are put together, these borders balance one another to form the total look.

BLOCK REQUIREMENTS

Through trial and error, I have found that a 12" square is a good finished block size not only for quilts, but also for accessories. Blocks can be used 2 ways in lap quilting: Method A, with 3" borders (sashing) on all four sides, producing an 18" square; or Method B, with four 12" blocks sewn together to form a 24" square. (See Block Requirement diagrams and charts.)

The quilt sizes listed below are standard. If you want your quilt to cover both the mattress and the box spring, or if your bed is an odd size, measure your bed accurately. Divide both the width and the length of your bed by your chosen block size, either 18" or 24", and multiply these numbers to come up with the necessary number of blocks. These measurements do not allow for take-up in quilting—about ½" per block.

Much depends on how you intend to use the quilt—as a total bed

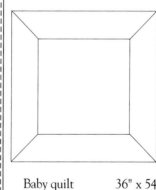

METHOD A

The following measurements apply to the 18"-square blocks (3"-wide borders attached to a 12" block).

Baby quilt	36" x 54"	6 blocks	2 across x 3 down
Afghan size	54" x 72"	12 blocks	3 across x 4 down
Twin size	54" x 90"	15 blocks	3 across x 5 down
Double size	72" x 90"	20 blocks	4 across x 5 down
Queen size	90" x 108"	30 blocks	5 across x 6 down
King size	108" x 108"	36 blocks	6 across x 6 down

Block Requirements

cover or folded as an accent at the end of the bed. If, after measuring the bed, you wish to alter the size of the finished quilt, change the width of the borders around each block, making wider and longer borders for a larger quilt or smaller borders to reduce the quilt size. If your border is increased by 1" around each block, 6" will be added to the width of a single bed quilt and 10" to its length. The quilt will then measure 60" x 100". Borders should be 4½" x 21" in this case. After layering and lap quilting, each block will be 20".

Plan ahead and measure carefully to give yourself a master plan; it is disappointing to end up with the wrong size quilt.

DRAFTING YOUR OWN DESIGN

You may find designing your own block rewarding. Do not be afraid to tackle this part of the quilting. Just being a quilter puts you in touch with the enormous possibility of potential designs you see around you every day. Here are the simple steps I follow:

- Decide on the division within the basic block. Is the pattern a natural four-patch or nine-patch, an asymmetrical or diagonal pattern, or a design best adapted to appliqué?
- Use graph paper to plot your design. Experiment with colored pencils for various alternatives.
- Enlarge the design to make an exact copy of the quilt block. Decide which templates will be needed. Add ¼" seam allowances to the templates and mark grain lines so that no bias edges are on the outside of the block. Cut a set of trial patterns from fabric and experiment with construction of the block.

ESTIMATING YARDAGE

Once you determine the number of blocks you will need, fabric must be measured or purchased. If you create blocks from whatever you have in scraps, you will be surprised at how little you'll need for one block. The time will come, of

METHOD B

Four 12"-square blocks sewn together make one 24"-square block. The blocks referred to in the following chart are, therefore, 24" squares.

Method B provides a different quilt measurement—a larger size in each instance. Always check your individual bed size for a happy outcome.

Baby quilt	48" x 48"	4 blocks	2 across x 2 down
Afghan size	48" x 72"	6 blocks	2 across x 3 down
Twin size	72" x 96"	12 blocks	3 across x 4 down
Double size	96" x 96"	16 blocks	4 across x 4 down
King size	120" x 120"	25 blocks	5 across x 5 down

Block Requirements

METHOD A

Block Material

Take the total amount given and divide by the number of fabrics you are using to determine separate yardage for each 12" block.

Baby quilt	6 blocks	1 yard
Afghan size	12 blocks	1½ yards
Twin size	15 blocks	2½ yards
Double size	20 blocks	3½ yards
Queen size	30 blocks	5 yards
King size	36 blocks	5½ yards

Border (Sashing) Material

Fabric needed for the 3"-wide border (sashing) around each block:

Baby quilt	24 rectangular borders	1½ yards
Afghan size	48 rectangular borders	3 yards
Twin size	60 rectangular borders	3½ yards
Double size	80 rectangular borders	4½ yards
Queen size	120 rectangular borders	6 yards
King size	144 rectangular borders	8 yards

Backing Material

Fabric needed for backing:

Baby quilt	6 blocks	1¾ yards
Afghan size	12 blocks	3½ yards
Twin size	15 blocks	4½ yards
Double size	20 blocks	6 yards
Queen size	30 blocks	8 yards
King size	36 blocks	10 yards

Estimating Yardage Table I

course, when you will want to buy new fabric, and the amounts given here will aid in that purchase. When in doubt, take your templates with you to the fabric store. Lay them on the fabric and determine how much of it you will need for a given block; then multiply that amount by the number of blocks of the design you will be making. Always buy an extra half yard.

Consider, too, the quilt's edging when purchasing fabric; you may need to purchase an extra yard for bias binding or a ruffle. In some cases, extra backing fabric is needed for perimeter blocks.

Determine separately the fabric needed to complete each component of your quilt—its blocks, its backing and, in Method A, its borders. The following tables for estimating yardage, on pages 16 and 17, assume a 45"-width fabric.

MAKING YOUR TEMPLATES

Templates are your guides for cutting the geometric shapes which, when sewn together, will form your blocks. Precision in drawing your templates and transferring them to cloth is essential. If the templates have a firm, hard edge, this step will

METHOD B

Method B is based on four 12"-square blocks sewn together to make one 24"-square block.

Block Material

Baby quilt size	16 (12") squares	4 blocks	2 yards
Afghan size	24 (12") squares	6 blocks	4½ yards
Twin size	48 (12") squares	12 blocks	8 yards
Double size	64 (12") squares	16 blocks	12 yards
King size	100 (12") squares	25 blocks	14 yards

Backing Material

Three squares of backing can be cut from every 2 yards of 45"-wide material. A fabric strip along the sides will result; this can be used in the front piecework or in another quilt. A striped or print backing can be pieced if you wish to make better use of the material width.

Baby quilt size	3 yards
Afghan size	4½ yards
Twin size	8 yards
Double size	11 yards
King size	16 yards

Estimating Yardage Table II

be easier. The geometric shapes may be transferred to templates in two ways. First, using a pencil and ruler, trace the exact lines onto tracing paper. Glue the tracing paper onto thin posterboard or cardboard with rubber cement and let dry overnight. Smooth clear adhesive-backed paper onto the top of each piece of cardboard to protect the patterns. Cut out each figure with paper scissors.

If you prefer, you can trace the shapes onto frosted vinyl, using a ruler and permanent pen, and then cut them out. This makes a perfect, long-lasting template. As you trace each pattern, mark the grain lines, the outside cutting edge, and the ¼" seam allowance onto the plastic. Label the right side of each template. Punch out the turns with a ⅛"-diameter hole punch. (See Template-Making Diagram.) You may also want to glue sandpaper to the backs of your templates. This will keep them from sliding on the fabric.

Quilts have been passed down from generation to generation. But the patterns for them have not fared as well; they probably wore out from constant use. Now, using vinyl and cardboard templates, you can pass on your patterns as well as your quilts.

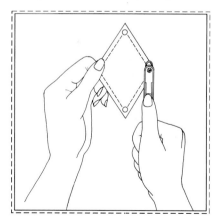

Template-Making Diagram

TEMPLATE PLACEMENT ON FABRIC

Excluding the selvage, carefully position the template on the fabric, noting how the pattern of the fabric falls within the boundaries of the seam lines. Hold the template firmly against the fabric and trace around it with a water-erasable pen, pencil, or a thin sliver of soap. When possible, borrow one straight edge from a previously marked pattern piece to save fabric. Cut out the fabric shape. Turn the fabric piece wrong side up and mark all corner turns indicated by the holes in the template.

I have found that a lapboard, with fine sandpaper covering the work surface, is ideal. The sandpaper prevents annoying fabric slippage, and this portable unit can be used in front of the TV or wherever you choose.

USING THE ROTARY CUTTER

Although scissors are our mainstay—and where would patchwork be without them?—consider the rotary cutter. The rotary cutter provides a precise cut and the

Rotary Cutting Diagram

advantage of cutting through 8 layers of fabric at 1 time. Working with a clear, thick quilters' ruler, a rotary cutter, and a companion mat board allows you to see and cut many consecutive layers. Several small pieces of self-adhesive sandpaper on the underside of the ruler will help prevent the ruler from sliding over the fabric while you are cutting long sections. Try to position the mat board so that you have access to all sides of it while cutting out your fabric. (See Rotary Cutter Diagram.)

The rotary cutter and mat can also be used for cutting out geometric shapes. The secret is using a transparent, right-angle triangle that has a thick edge. The triangle is less cumbersome than a large ruler when you are working with small shapes. Match the grain lines of the template and fabric and then position the triangle on top. Use the rotary cutter with the blade against the edge of the triangle. With some shapes, such as parallelograms or trapezoids, you must layer the fabric with all the right sides up to ensure that the pieces are uniform. With equal-sided shapes, such as squares or diamonds, you can layer fabric back to back or front to front.

PATTERN ENLARGEMENT FOR APPLIQUÉD PIECES

How to enlarge an appliqué pattern is a handy bit of information for a quilter to know. (See pages 30-34 for a discussion of appliqué techniques.) There may be a bank logo, a picture of a favorite pet, a camp emblem, or another unique design that needs to be enlarged at some time. Most of us are not artists, and we need help to scale up a design. There are at least six different methods we can use to tackle this task.

The first five methods rely on mechanical means:

1. The opaque projector is an apparatus that allows you to use the actual picture to be altered. It projects and enlarges the image so that you can trace it.

2. The overhead projector relies on a transparency of the image to be enlarged. To make a transparency, use a special pen and draw the outline of the desired object on an acetate sheet (available at office supply stores). Place it on a light platform, and the image will be projected.

3. There are small inexpensive enlargers that work well in the home. To use one of these machines, your design must be small.

4. Using a slide projector and screen is another possibility. You may already have a 35-mm slide in your collection that you would like to use. If not, you can take a picture of the object you wish to reproduce and have a slide made of it.

5. The pantograph is also an intriguing tool for changing design sizes. It is one of the oldest enlarging tools and is based on a set of overlapping hinged beams. These beams must be tightly anchored to a table. A pointer pin is attached at one end of the tool and a pencil or pen attached to the other end. You simply trace the original artwork with the pointer pin, and the pencil attached to the other end makes an enlarged copy.

Most schools and libraries have these five tools and are willing to let you use them. The projectors and small enlargers work best when set on a table with wheels in a darkened room. Then the size of the image can be varied by moving the machine forward or backward.

6. Using a grid or graph is another way to change a design size, for those of us who are not mechanically inclined. When a grid overlays a design, the design can be copied square by square onto a larger grid, thus enlarging the design. By coding the squares across and down one side, it's easy to keep track of any changes. Gridded paper for enlarging is available at most craft and fabric stores, or you can use graph paper and outline the desired grid size.

After enlarging a design, there are occasions in quilting when we need a means to see through fabric or paper to trace or transfer lines. Placing it over a light source can help us do this with ease. The light source can be a sunny window, a light under a glass tabletop, or a homemade light box. To make a light box, position a light source (either a light bulb or a fluorescent lamp) inside a box with a piece of plexiglass resting on top. Lay your pattern on the plexiglass and place the tracing paper on top of the pattern. ◆

FIRST, PIECE THE BLOCKS

PATCHWORK PIECING

A picture of the finished block kept close by will certainly facilitate this step. Whether sewing by hand or machine, the same ¼" seam allowance is used. Study the pattern and find the smallest pieces; these will be sewn together first. Is your block a four patch, nine patch, or one that depends on a center assembly such as Log Cabin or Formal Garden? Break each block down into sections and know how it is constructed.

HAND PIECING

If you choose to piece your block by hand, be sure you have a proper knot in a single strand of thread. (Quilting thread provides additional strength.) Align the pieces with the right sides and raw edges together and pin in place. Take 2 or 3 stitches, or as many stitches as possible, before pulling the needle through the fabric. Each time you insert the needle again, take a

backstitch to lock your stitches. End each seam with a double-loop knot. Your stitching should stop at the ¼" turn.

MACHINE PIECING
Know Your Sewing Machine

Do you have good rapport with your sewing machine? Are you on the same wavelength? Read your manual thoroughly and keep it close to the sewing area. Become familiar with the terminology of all the machine's parts. Then when you call the repairman, you won't have to refer to a part as the "thing-a-mabob" or "whatcha-ma-call-it." If you are entitled to private instructions with the purchase of your machine, take full advantage of them.

Know the most popular presser feet available for your machine. Learn to use your attachments. Even if you have had a tendency to shy away from that box of intricate devices, remember that taking the time to explore them may open up new sewing avenues.

If you sew with an all-purpose foot, check the distance from the needle to the outside edge of the foot; you may find that it is ¼", making it a good guide for seam allowance. If not, masking tape can be placed on the throat plate ¼" from the needle, as can a magnetic attachment available at sewing notions counters. The ability to sew a true ¼" seam allowance comes with practice; do not expect perfection at first. Just as in any new learning experience, trial and error is involved, so be patient. You'll learn gradually that some materials sew together more easily than others. Here's a hint: Be conscious of the diagonal bias lines of triangles and avoid stretching them while sewing.

One of the most important parts of the sewing machine is the needle. When you are sewing frequently, needles need to be replaced often. Don't tug on the needle when you snip your threads. Angle your threads away from the presser foot before you snip. This will prevent you from bending or breaking your needle. (You may want to save your old needles; they make great nails with which to hang light-weight objects on the wall.)

If you are in the habit of sewing over pins at a right angle, be my guest. I do pin sets together in the middle to anchor them, and I also place pins at intersections, but I do not sew over them.

Use a mercerized, cotton-covered, polyester thread that is compatible with your fabric for machine piecing. A neutral shade such as beige or gray works well with many blocks. Take the time to load several bobbins, and you will always be ready to sew.

Where is your machine placed? If you have to plunk your machine on the kitchen table and rush through a project in order to make way for dinner, rethink your plan. Isn't there a corner in the bedroom, hall area, or even the dining room that could be screened off when not in use? The machine should be available at all times, not hidden in a case.

Have you considered using a stenographers' chair while working at the sewing machine? You can adjust the seat height (20" is right for me). The wheels allow you to scoot from the machine to the iron. No matter what chair you sit in, it should be high enough so that you can look down on the throat plate and the needle.

Hints for Care of Your Sewing Machine

- Keep your machine covered when not in use.

- Use a thread of good quality; poor-quality and inexpensive thread hinders the mechanism.

- Keep plenty of bobbins loaded; check plastic bobbins for any irregularities.

- Oil your machine, following the guidelines in your maintenance book.

- Keep the area around the feed dogs and bobbin case free of lint.

- Always turn the handwheel toward you; do not push or turn it in a backward motion.

Basic Patchwork Piecing

Patchwork can be the perfect place to practice your machine stitching, since you will be sewing many short, straight lines. I recommend a moderate speed and a visual point of control, whether it's the needle, masking tape on the throat plate, or a marked seam allowance. It takes a keen eye to navigate a repeated motion. (It isn't necessary to backstitch when machine piecing if the seams cross.)

Curved piecing on the machine can be achieved with practice and patience. When machine-piecing blocks like Virginia's Choice and Drunkard's Path, hold the concave piece against the throat plate and gently swing the convex edge around to meet it, stitching on the seam line. Pinning the midpoint before sewing will help you stay on target as you make the swing. (See Curved Piecing Diagrams.)

Machine-piecing the inside right angle of a point, such as the 90° angles on a star block, also requires close attention. Carefully sew up to the ¼" turn (point A); stop and backstitch. (See Set-In Piecing Diagram I.) This allows the seam to be

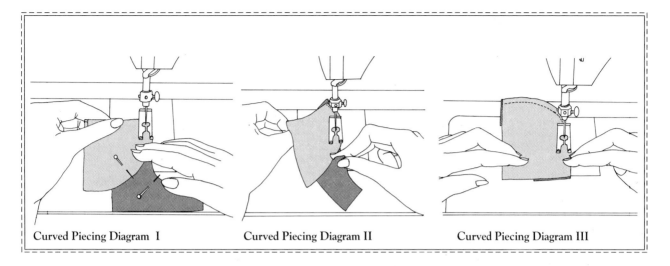

Curved Piecing Diagram I   Curved Piecing Diagram II   Curved Piecing Diagram III

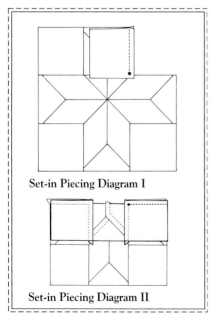

Set-in Piecing Diagram I

Set-in Piecing Diagram II

free floating. Align the other side of the corner square, right sides together, with the next star point. Sew from point A to the outside edge. (See Set-In Piecing Diagrams.)

Piecing Four-Patch Blocks

The basic four-patch patterns are each made up of 4(6") blocks that are constructed in a similar manner and are then stitched together to make a 12" block.

You'll be tempted to put each of the 4 small blocks together independently, but wait! You'll save time and have a better alignment if you take an assembly line approach.

If each of these quarter sections has a triangle connected to a trapezoid, for instance, make those four connections in a continuous manner. Put your 4 sets of triangles and trapezoids together by laying them out, right sides touching, aligning their raw edges, and then pinning. Slide the first set through the machine; sew on air for a moment; lift the presser foot; and ease another set through. (See Continuous Piecing Diagram on page 24.) When all 4 seams are made, cut stitching between sets. Then add the other pieces needed to make each quarter section.

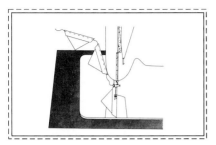

Continuous Piecing Diagram

Connect quarter sections according to the block design. A ⅛" discrepancy at the seam can be fudged, but anything smaller or larger than ¼" means back to the cutting board. If you cut your pieces too large or take too small a seam allowance, your piecework will "grow," and you'll lose the points on stars. It is natural at first to take too large a seam allowance; but if you've done that, or have cut your pieces too small, your quarter section will shrink.

There are exceptions to the quarter-section assembly. One is Road to Oklahoma, where it is best to work in rectangles due to the trapezoids. The following are special tips for assembling the four-patch patterns.

Rail Fence— Lay out 8 sets of 2 rectangles each and sew them using the continuous piecing method described above. Match each set of 2 to another set and sew, resulting in 4 squares made up of 4 rectangles each. Press seams in an outward direction and check quarter section size. Sew 2 quarter sections together; repeat with second set. Now pin the 2 half sections together, staggering seams in the center, and sew. (See Quick Strip Method for Piecing Rectangles on page 29 for an alternative way of piecing the Rail Fence block.)

King's X— Lay out 4 sets of 2 trapezoids each and sew them together using the continuous piecing method described above. Sew triangles to each of the 8 short sides, letting the same amount of dog-ear extend from each of the triangles. Consult block diagram and set the quarter sections in the proper arrangement; sew and press all seams in a clockwise direction so that they will automatically stagger.

Kansas Trouble— Lay out 16 sets of 2 triangles each and sew together to form squares (see section on Quick-Piecing Method on page 27); then sew 8 sets of 2 squares each together to form rectangles. Add a dark triangle to the end of each rectangle; the shape that results will be referred to as a "star section." Add a square to the 1 end of each of 4 star sections. Attach the remaining 4 star sections to a triangle; then add to the triangle the 4 star sections to which squares were attached. You will have 4 pieced triangles. Each is now attached to a solid triangle to form a quarter section.

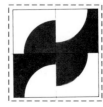

Drunkard's Path— Place a pin at the midpoint of each curve; align pins as pieces are joined. (See Curved Piecing Diagrams on page 23.) If pins are not aligning at midpoint, ease fabric to the end of the seam. The bottom fabric shifts to the left and the top comes to meet the raw edge. Clip seams to press them outward; notch them to press in.

Coffee Cup—
Sew together 2 light-colored squares. Appliqué handle to the rectangle formed. Piece together quarter sections according to the block design and assemble as a four patch.

Cube Accent—
For each quarter section, form trapezoids by sewing dark triangles at outer edges to parallelograms in corners (4 per quarter section). Sew the trapezoids to the center square by pivoting with the needle in the material. Or sew sides only up to the ¼" seam allowance, leaving angled seams to be sewn in a separate step.

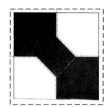

Bow Tie—
Sew the short side of one pentagon to the side of the center square; sew the short side of another pentagon to the opposite side of the square. Pivot the remaining two pentagons into place at the seam intersection. The needle must be in the seam to hold this turn in place. Pivot at the 135° angle; it will not work at right angles.

Piecing Log Cabin Blocks
The basic Log Cabin block and its variations rely on adding contrasting rectangles to the central square. Cut all strips the same width, as indicated by the pattern. Machine-stitch the shortest strip to the central square, trim ends even with the square, and crease the seam to the outside. Then add the other strips one at a time in a continuous circle. Keep adding strips until there are 5 on all 4 sides of the center square.

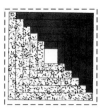

Log Cabin—
To form each circle of strips, sew two light strips, then two dark strips. You may use two different light fabrics as long as both contrast to the dark fabric.

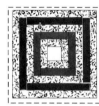

Log Cabin Variation #1—Sew the same fabric on all four sides for each circular row, alternating fabrics with each row. This pattern is sometimes called Around the World.

Log Cabin Variation #2—Alternate fabrics with each strip added. The resulting Courthouse Steps pattern will have opposite sides of the same fabrics.

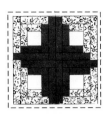

Log Cabin Four Patch—Make quarter sections by adding 2 rows of contrasting fabrics to each of the center squares. Assemble the 4 sections to form 1 block.

Piecing Nine-Patch Blocks

The nine-patch blocks are sewn in the assembly line manner described for four-patch blocks (page 23). Sew 3 sets of 2 patches each together in a continuous manner; clip apart. Then add one patch to each set. Staggering seams, sew together these 3 rows of 3 squares to complete block.

Piecing Combination Blocks

Moon Over the Mountain and Four Seasons—Sew the 3 moon sections to the 3 sky sections, forming 3 triangles. Adding mountain triangle, sew 2 sets of 2 triangles, forming 2 large triangles. Sew large triangles together to

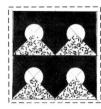

complete block. Be sure to stagger moon-to-sky seams so that they alternate and will connect perfectly. (See Moon Over the Mountain Block Diagram.)

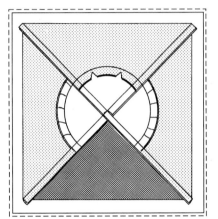

Moon Over the Mountain Block Diagram

Grandmother's Fan and Dresden Plate—Sew small wedges together in 2s first, then in 4s, etc. Attach quarter circle as in Drunkard's Path instructions (page 24); attach rickrack or lace to the circular raw edge. It can then be turned under, hiding

raw edge and revealing half of the rickrack or lace. Place the fan or plate on a 12½"-square of foundation material and slipstitch in-the-ditch to secure. Handbaste the opening of Dresden Plate under ¼" so that the contrasting center circle can be slipped underneath and slipstitched in place.

Monkey Wrench—Sew together the center four-patch square; then add 4 triangles to the sides of the square. Make sure that the same amount of dog-ear extends from each side. Repeat this procedure with the 2 remaining sets of triangles.

Hexagon Flowerette—Connect the pieces of each vertical row by machine. You will have 2 rows of 3 pieces, 2 rows of 4 pieces, and a center row of 5 pieces. Now pivot one row into the next. (See Hexagon Piecing Diagram.) Baste under ¼" seam allowance and appliqué the flowerette to a 12½" foundation.

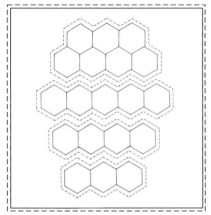

Hexagon Piecing Diagram

Spider Web— Sew a trapezoid to each of the triangles. Sew these larger triangles together in sections of 4. Connect these to form an octagon; the seam will be at an angle. Attach the corner triangles to square off the block.

Cross & Crown— Assemble the 4 corner patches; attach 1 to each side of a rectangle. Form the center row and sew it to the 2 larger rectangles.

Pieced Little Dutch Boy— Sew triangle to pentagon and add another pentagon to form body. Appliqué an arm to each triangle before sewing these to the body. Appliqué both feet to 1 triangle and then sew the 3 triangles into place. Add triangles to complete block.

Pieced Little Dutch Girl— Sew triangle to pentagon; attach trapezoid. Add triangle to each side. Appliqué the foot to 1 triangle and then add the 3 triangles. Add corner triangles. Appliqué the arm; if a hand is desired, fold a 1" square in half, find the midpoint of the side opposite the fold, and crease the folded corners toward it, forming a triangle. Consider adding lace to the front of the hat.

TIME-SAVING METHODS FOR MACHINE PIECING

Quick-Piecing Method for Turning Triangles into Squares

Whenever 2 identical right-angled triangles are to be sewn together to form a square several times in a block, you can use a shortcut method of machine piecing. This Quick-Piecing Method will save a great deal of time, especially when you are repeating the same block many times in a quilt.

Simply lay out the two contrasting fabrics you are using, right sides together. Count the number of squares made up of 2 triangles that are included in your block, and trace the triangle template that number of times onto the wrong side of the fabric, as shown in Triangles into Squares Piecing Diagram I.

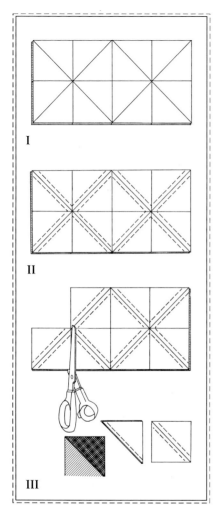

Triangles into Squares Piecing Diagrams

Using a ruler, carefully draw another line ¼" from and on both sides of each diagonal line. (See Triangles into Squares Piecing Diagram II.) This new set of lines represents your sewing line. Machine-stitch along it continuously.

After machine stitching, cut the fabric along the lines originally drawn, as shown in Triangles into Squares Piecing Diagram III. Your triangles are sewn into squares before they are even cut!

Turning Triangles into Pieced Triangles

With one minor difference, the above method can be used when 2 right-angled triangles are to be joined to form a larger *triangle*. In this case, mark your sewing line on both sides of only one continuous diagonal line. Sew along broken lines, as shown in Triangles into Triangles Piecing Diagram I. Cut apart on *all* solid lines.

To form squares from these pieced triangles, align raw edges, stagger seams, and sew together using ¼" seam allowances. (See Triangles into Triangles Piecing Diagram II.)

Quick Strip Method

Strip patchwork is the technique of sewing several long strips of contrasting fabrics together to form a striped band (Quick Strip-Piecing Diagram I). The striped band is

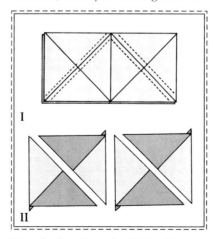

Triangles Into Triangles Piecing Diagram

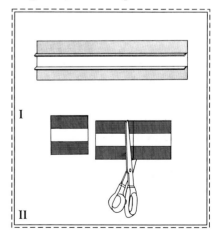

Quick Strip-Piecing Diagrams

then cut into segments that can be arranged in new patterns (Quick Strip-Piecing Diagram II). This method of piecing fabric is a real time-saver when several squares or rectangles of the same width are to be joined in the same color sequence.

Quick Strip Method for Piecing Four-Patch and Nine-Patch Blocks

To form a simple four patch, stack 2 contrasting, but compatible, fabrics with right sides together. Cut 4 strips (2 from each fabric) the width equal to 1 side of your square (with seam allowances) and 45" long, on the crosswise or lengthwise grain of the fabric. With right sides together, sew 2 strips of contrasting fabrics together along long edge with ¼" seams. Repeat for the other 2 strips. Open each strip and press the seam toward the darker fabric.

Align these 2 strips, right sides together, with colors reversed and seams staggered. (See Quick Four-Patch Piecing Diagram I.) On the back of the fabric, measure and mark off segments equal to the side of your square with a solid line. (Be

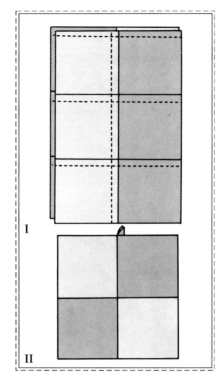

Quick Four-Patch Piecing Diagrams

sure to include seam allowances in this measurement.) Now mark a broken line ¼" to the left (or right—be consistent) of each solid line, as shown in Quick Four-Patch Piecing Diagram II; stitch along each broken line. Cut on the solid lines to reveal your four-patch squares.

This technique works for a nine patch as well. Sew 1 set of bands of dark, light, dark, and then sew another of light, dark, light. Then proceed, following the instructions for the four patch.

Quick Strip Method for Piecing Rectangles

Stack 2 contrasting, but compatible, fabrics with right sides together. Cut 2 strips (1 from each fabric) the width of your rectangle (with seam allowances) and 45" long, on the crosswise or lengthwise grain of your fabric. Sew 1 long edge of these strips together with a ¼" seam (Quick Rectangle-Piecing Diagram I). Mark and cut apart in

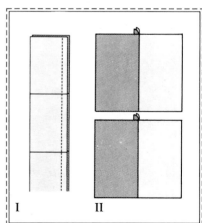

Quick Rectangle-Piecing Diagrams

segments equal to the length of your rectangle (with seam allowances). Press the seam allowance toward the darker fabric (Quick Rectangle-Piecing Diagram II). To expand this idea, as in the blocks of the quilt *Rail Fence* (page 24), sew a band with the desired number of colors and cut apart.

APPLIQUÉ

The term appliqué is from a French word meaning to apply (as a decoration or ornament) to a larger surface.

Potential appliqué designs are all around us—in nature, children's coloring books, simple folded-paper cutouts, and of course, in quilts from the past. A study of quilting would not be complete without a study of appliqué. Since there are many ways to appliqué and since we all hold a needle and handle fabric differently, we must test and discover our own favorite method. The severity of the curve or point will often determine the method we use.

Appliqué without Seam Allowance

The simplest form of appliqué is the figure cut without any seam allowance. The edges may be secured by hand or by machine. This method was most often seen in early 20th-century Dutch Girl quilts in which black embroidery thread was used to form very close buttonhole stitches around the figures. (See Buttonhole-Stitched Appliqué Diagram.) A certain amount of fraying would start once the figures were handled and used, but eventually it would cease and form a decorative uniform edge.

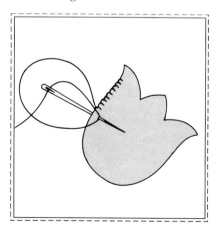

Buttonhole-Stitched Appliqué Diagram

Machine Appliqué

The satin stitch on a sewing machine can form a very neat, tight edging, as shown in the Satin-Stitched Appliqué Diagram.

Satin-Stitched Appliqué Diagram

The thread color can vary here—a contrast to accent or a match to blend with the appliqué figure. Before sewing, however, secure the cutout figure in position with a spray adhesive or stick glue. This prevents the cutout from shifting while you are sewing. If you are appliquéing a figure to a single thickness of fabric, it helps to have a stabilizer underneath, because machine satin stitches tend to draw the fabric.

The open embroidery presser foot or an all-purpose presser foot can be aligned with the raw edge to provide a stitching guide. To achieve the proper width and length of your zigzag stitch, always do a test sample first. With these types of presser feet, it is important to note the position of the needle at right-angle turns. For outside right-angle turns, pivot with the needle on the outside or right side. For inside right-angle turns, pivot with the needle on the inside or left side.

You will need to alter the width of the satin stitch as you sew, to make adjustments for acute corners such as those found in star or leaf points. Narrow the satin stitch as you approach any sharp angles. Turn and slowly widen the stitches as you move away from the point area. When finished, pull the loose top thread to the back of the fabric and tie off. To give elevation and emphasis to the satin stitch, lay a narrow piece of cord along the edge and satin-stitch over it.

If your sewing machine has a blind hem stitch, you might use it to appliqué. Set the presser foot very close to the folded edge. Sew a series of small stitches on the foundation fabric or block, and then catch the turned-under edge of the appliqué figure with one short zigzag stitch. Use a clear polyfilament thread to disguise any stitches.

Appliqué with Seam Allowance

Most forms of hand appliqué have a seam allowance or ¼" extension that needs to be turned under to form a smooth, finished edge. A template that includes seam allowances is used to cut out the appliquéd figure. (If the template is made from plastic, you can see through it to position it according to the design of the fabric.)

A second template, without seam allowances, can also be a good tool. Trace around it on the foundation fabric to make a guide for turning under the raw edges of the appliquéd figure. This will also show you where to position the appliqué. Another way to make a guide for turning under raw edges is to trace around the template without seam allowances on the appliqué figure itself.

If you place this second template on top of the appliqué figure and iron the seam allowances back over the template, you form a crease.

This shows you how far to turn under the raw edge. Spray starch helps set this pressed curve. (If you use this technique, make sure the template is made of cardboard or freezer paper—not plastic.)

Appliqué seams are treated in a variety of ways. The ¼" seam allowance can be basted under with a contrasting thread. (Work with the back of the figure facing you and the knot on the front for easy removal.) On curved seams, clip any concave seams and notch the fullness out of convex seams. A simple machine staystitch sewn right next to the seam line adds weight to the appliqué figure and makes the turn-under easier and more exact.

You may wish to add a stem stitch worked by hand along the finished edge (¼" from the raw edge). This will form a neat edge after the seam allowance is turned under.

Double appliqué is actually a double thickness of fabric—the appliqué figure and a facing. Align the right sides of the appliqué figure and the facing and sew all the way around them with a ¼" seam allowance. Trim and clip all seams for a smooth finish. Snip a small

Double Appliqué Diagram

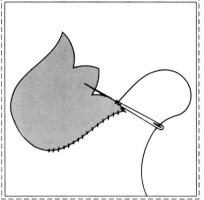

Slipstitched Appliqué Diagram

opening in the facing, as shown in Double Appliqué Diagram. Turn the figure right side out; press flat before applying the figure to the foundation fabric.

Sewing the Appliqué

The slipstitch is the usual stitch for attaching appliqué figures to a foundation or base fabric. (A whipstitch doesn't work because loose threads will catch and wear out.) A proper slipstitch is worked from right to left. The needle is pulled up through the block or foundation fabric and catches only a few threads of the folded edge of the appliqué figure. Each time the needle is inserted in the block, it should be under the top thread on the edge of the appliqué figure. (See Slipstitched Appliqué Diagram.) This keeps the thread from angling. You should have long single strands of thread showing on the back, but very little, if any, thread should be visible on the front.

Once the figures are slipstitched in place, you can add an accent line of stem stitching at the very edge.

The appliqué figure can also be attached by basting the figure in position and then, with the point of the needle, turning the seam allowance under as you slipstitch the figure in place. This method takes practice and careful basting. It helps to draw the figure first on the foundation or block as a guide.

Using a close, tiny running stitch at the very edge of the turned-under seam allowance is another simple, yet effective, way to appliqué. Use thread that blends with the fabric.

The above techniques can also be used with reverse appliqué, Hawaiian appliqué, and shadow trapunto. These are in the category of novelty work and can be very effective used alone or mixed with other techniques.

Single-Surface Appliqué

One problem that occurs in appliqué is that as layers are added, bulk is produced, making hand quilting difficult. In this cutaway method, only slight overlapping occurs where colors meet. To try single-surface appliqué, just follow this step-by-step procedure. (Illustrations give steps for machine-appliquéd pieces, but the same steps are applicable to hand-appliquéd pieces.)

1. Preparing. Enlarge the design if the original is not the desired size.

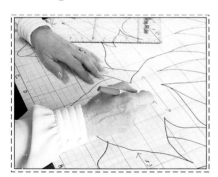

2. Coding. Number each piece in the order to be applied, larger pieces first, then smaller pieces. Indicate fabric color and grain line. This becomes your master paper foundation.

3. Making Templates. Place paper foundation on light box, wrong side up. Place freezer paper, dull side up, over it. Using an indelible pen, trace each shape and transfer any codes. Cut out.

4. Cutting the Pieces. Using a dry iron on a warm setting, press the freezer paper template with the shiny side against the wrong side of the desired fabric. Cut fabric ½" outside edge of template.

5. Positioning Templates. Layer paper and foundation fabric (right sides up) on light box. Remove template from fabric piece and pin piece to foundation fabric. Trace shape onto fabric piece.

6. Sewing. Machine-stitch the appliqué piece to the foundation along the outline. Use a straight, standard stitch. (Complete steps 6 through 12 for any one template before positioning the next template.)

7. Trimming. Trim the material extending beyond the straight stitching. With pins, mark the areas where the pieces will overlap.

9. Appliquéing. Satin-stitch on the edge of the figure, covering the straight stitching. Gradually narrow your satin stitch as you come to a point and increase it as you move away from the point.

11. Separating the Fabrics. Pull the foundation fabric away from the fabric piece you just appliquéd.

8. Pinning Paper. Pin a piece of typing paper underneath foundation fabric under appliqué piece. Test a satin stitch on a sample fabric to determine desired width of zigzag stitch.

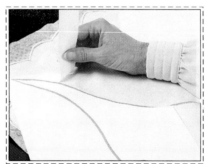

10. Tearing Away Paper. Carefully tear away the typing paper. Remove any small fragments of the paper caught in the stitching.

12. Cutting Away Fabric. Carefully cut away the foundation fabric underneath the appliqué, trimming up to the satin stitching. Use appliqué scissors to achieve a close trim.

FINAL STEPS IN BLOCK ASSEMBLY

Eliminating Bulky Intersections

Where seams join at right angles and at star intersections, there is always an excessive amount of bulk created by the seam allowances. This can cause the front of the block to be raised on one side of the seam. At last a solution! I picked up this technique in Billings, Montana, so I call it my Billings Bonus.

Pressing

Having ready access to an iron as you work is the ideal situation. Thumb creasing is only temporary. Never press open the seams in piecework. This would weaken the piecework and make it more vulnerable.

After the block is assembled, crease and steam-press seams on the back toward the darker fabric patch when possible; this keeps the seam allowance from showing through a lighter piece. Turn over the block and press on the top side to eliminate any creases.

Patchwork Accuracy

Check your pieced section for accuracy. As you piece your block, compare each small section to a master template. Your master template is a template cut the size of a small pieced section within the block. If the completed section has shrunk before your very eyes, check

1. Sewing. Sew the intersection with closed staggered seams (raw edges of seam allowances going in different directions).

2. Ripping. With a pin or seam ripper, rip out only the stitches in the intersecting seam allowances.

3. Positioning Seams. Position the seams in a concentric circle.

Eliminating Bulky Intersections

to see if the seam allowances are too large, the templates are incorrect, or the fabric sections are cut too small.

By the same token, an oversized section may be the result of seam allowances that are too small, incorrect templates, or fabric pieces cut too large. Constant checking with the master template as the block is in progress will help you avoid using the seam ripper. The use of the seam ripper, however, is not a catastrophe. I believe that it builds character and cautions you against making the same mistake twice—at least this is the theory.

Marking the Seam Allowance

Once your blocks are pieced or appliquéd, the next step is mandatory! Cut a perfect 12" square from plastic or posterboard. Center this on the back of your block and trace around it, marking a ¼" seam allowance on all four sides. Do not cut this off; it is a guide to follow when attaching borders or sewing blocks to one another. Even when the same fabrics and the same patterns are used, blocks will vary in size. Check for true right angles and ample ¼" seam allowances around

the perimeter of each block. In a sampler quilt, block sizes may be quite different, so don't skip this important step. Now, take a deep breath and correct any mistakes you might discover; it will save considerable aggravation later.

The lap-quilting process really begins once all the blocks are pieced. Remove any remaining fabric markings with a clean damp sponge and trim any dog-ears. If using Method A, refer to section on Attaching Borders to Blocks. If using Method B, join blocks in four-block sections to make a larger square block, as shown on page 15 in Chapter 2. Enjoy your patchwork while anticipating your next step—the actual quilting.

ATTACHING BORDERS TO BLOCKS (Method A)

Mitered Borders

If the design for your quilt calls for borders, you will find that a neat, mitered border frames each block beautifully. (See Mitered-Borders Assembly Diagram IV.) Varying the colors and sizes of the borders from block to block can also help

you achieve a wide variety of effects, but one thing remains constant: the border for any given block must be the same width on all four sides.

Calculation of Dimensions for Mitered Borders: Decide on the width of the mitered border. The length of the border is equal to *twice* the width (including seam allowances) plus the width of the block. An easy formula to follow:

```
  2 x  width of border (including
          seam allowances)
  +  width of block

  =  length of border
```
For example, a 3"-wide border has the following measurements:

```
  2 x 3½" (½" for seam allowances)
  = 7" + 12" (width of block)
  = 19"
```

Cut your 4 border strips 3½" x 19". If you are planning a double mitered border, sew the two fabrics together in a long band before cutting the 4 borders. Cut all borders on the straight of grain, since crosswise grain tends to have more give at the corners.

Perfect Mitering: Follow these steps carefully for a perfect mitered corner:

Step 1: Cut 4 border strips, after calculating their dimensions as described above. Place 1 border strip on the edge of the block, right sides together, so that equal amounts extend from each side (Mitered-Borders Assembly Diagram I).

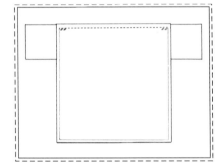

Mitered-Borders Assembly Diagram I

Step 2: Align the right side of 1 border with the right side of the block, so that equal amounts of the border strip extend from each end of the block. Begin sewing ¼" in from the raw edge of the block, following the previously marked seam line. Backstitch to the seam line and stitch to other end, stopping at the opposite seam line; backstitch to secure. Continue to add the other three borders in the same way. Notice the loose right angle that occurs at each corner.

Mitered-Borders Assembly Diagram II

Step 3: Let borders extend outward with overlapping. Each outside edge becomes a guide to trim off the excess of the other borders. There is a perfect right angle overlap at each corner (Mitered-Borders Assembly Diagram II).

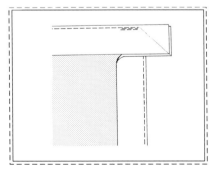

Mitered-Borders Assembly Diagram III

Step 4: Fold together the right sides of adjacent borders, forming a triangle at the corners, and draw a straight line from inside the backstitching point to the outside corner on the border fabric. Machine-sew along this line, backstitching at the inside and sewing outward to the tip (Mitered-Borders Assembly Diagram III). Trim a ¼" seam allowance and press seams between block and border in the same direction, either

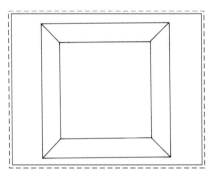

Mitered-Borders Assembly Diagram IV

toward the block (if you want to quilt on the border) or away from the block (if you want to quilt inside the block, close to the border). (See Mitered-Border Assembly Diagram IV.) Press the diagonal, mitered seam in a clockwise direction on each corner. Save all those leftover triangles for your next quilt.

Strip Addition: An Alternative to Mitered Borders

If your design calls for borders, but you don't want mitered border corners, strips can frame your blocks in a number of ways.

The first method calls for two strips cut the width of your choice and the length of the block. These are sewn to opposite sides of the block. To the remaining sides, add strips cut long enough to include the width of the first strips sewn. (See Block Border Alternatives Diagram I.)

A similar effect can be achieved by adding strips sewn in the Log Cabin fashion, starting on one side and adding strips in a circular fashion. (See Block Border Alternatives Diagram II.)

Adding square accents to corners is another effective border treatment. Add strips to opposite sides first (Block Border Alternatives Diagram III.) Then sew square to 1 end of each of the remaining 2 strips. Pin corners and find the exact placement of the opposite square before sewing in place (Block Border Alternatives Diagram IV.) Stagger seams for the strongest connection. ◆

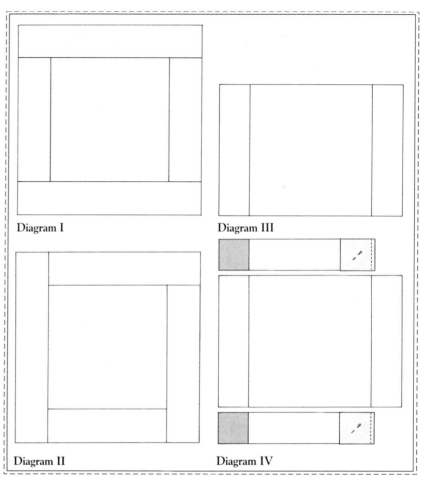

Diagram I

Diagram III

Diagram II

Diagram IV

Block Border Alternatives

SELECTION OF QUILTING DESIGNS

The stencil or quilting design is the line you follow when you are quilting. These lines are applied to the block after it is pieced or appliquéd but before it is basted to the batting and backing.

To decide on your quilting design, evaluate your block. Does it have direction? Do you want to emphasize star points? What is the overall feeling? There are two types of stencil or quilting lines—contrary and compatible.

Contrary lines create a new secondary design. They don't follow the lines of the piecework or appliqué, but should enhance and not detract. For example, use a fan design on top of a log cabin square or a feather wreath with a star patchwork pattern. Be creative. Don't overlook the possibilities that lie in the shapes of everyday items around your house. Cookie cutters, cups and saucers, and even children's toys can be your instant templates.

Original quilting designs can set your quilt apart and make it truly your own.

Compatible, or outline, quilting is the traditonal form of quilting. These quilting stitches echo the lines created by seams or turned-under edges and beautifully accentuate the geometric piecing. Quite often it is only necessary to quilt on 1 side of a seam line inside the block. Try to choose the side that does not have the seam allowance, and you'll avoid unnecessary bulk. Quilting lines should run ⅛" to ¼" from the seam line; remember that the seam line is your guide and will help you to quilt in a parallel line. The further you get from that line, the easier it will be for your line of stitches to become crooked. I do not recommend quilting in-the-ditch, exactly on the connecting seam line; any quilting stitches there are obscured. If you like the look of quilting ¼" from the seam line, try placing ¼"-wide masking tape along the seam after the block

is basted and quilting along the opposite edge of the tape. Then remove the tape and place it on the next area to be quilted.

The secret to lap quilting is keeping at least ½" to 1" around each side of a block unquilted. A quilting design such as cross-hatching, which is handsome for pillows and place mats, does not work well on the borders of lap-quilting blocks that will eventually be connected, because the lines extend out to the raw edges, preventing assembly of the blocks.

When planning your quilting design, keep in mind that the quilting pattern should flow from the center outward, and the amount of quilting in the separate sections must be consistent.

MARKING THE QUILTING PATTERN

The next step is transferring the stencil designs to your blocks. These designs become your path to follow in making your quilting stitches. The way they are placed on the fabric is very important; they must be easy to follow for quilting, yet simple to remove once the quilting is completed.

First, make sure each block has been well pressed and will lie flat. Choose a marking implement—a fabric pen or pencil, a sliver of soap, water-erasable pen, soapstone marker, or tailors' chalk—and test it to be sure it can be easily removed from the fabric.

Once you've chosen the quilting pattern you want, there are several methods of transferring it to the fabric. Try placing light-colored fabric directly on the top of the dark-lined patterns. If you can see the pattern through the fabric, simply trace the pattern directly onto the fabric with your marking device.

Unless your fabric is very light in color, though, you will need to trace the pattern onto paper with a heavy marker, place the paper under the fabric, and find a way to illuminate the paper and fabric from behind. A sunny window works well, as does a glass-topped table with a light below it. Or you can improvise a light box from a cardboard box by putting a hole in the bottom or side for a light and taping a piece of glass to the top.

You can also make cardboard or plastic templates. Position the templates on the fabric and trace around the designs, using either a continuous line or dots. Also popular today are precut stencils or stencils that you make yourself from plastic.

If you prefer, cut the stencil shape out of self-adhesive paper, and apply it after the block is basted. The shape will adhere to the fabric while you're quilting around it; then simply remove it and attach it to the next area to be quilted. This method eliminates the use of pen or pencil marks. Remember that special shapes cut from masking tape or self-adhesive paper should not be left on the fabric for long periods of time, or they may become difficult to remove.

THE THREE B'S—BATTING, BACKING, AND BASTING
Batting and Backing

The stencil-marked block is your pattern for cutting the batting and backing. Whether you have added a border to a 12" block (Method A) or have sewn four blocks together without borders (Method B), your dimensions should already include outside seam allowances, so there is no need to cut backing larger than your block.

There are many different types of batting available today. Polyester and perfected cotton batting can be fluffy, or flat and compact. It gives you great freedom; large areas can be left unquilted since the batting will not separate and get lumpy with washing. There is also a thin, flat fleece batting in combinations of cotton and polyester or varieties of wool. Invest in a good-quality batting to ensure the longevity of your quilt and handiwork.

Backing fabric is of primary importance in lap quilting. Muslin is often used because it highlights the quilting stitches, and it is inexpensive. Dark-colored backings are not the best choice for a beginner using white quilting thread, because the stitches are prominent. Print fabrics tend to hide quilting stitches completely, but they help to hide the handmade connections on the back.

Basting

Since you do not want these 3 layers—block, batting, backing—to shift while you are quilting, it is necessary at this point to baste them together. Basting is an important step, regardless of the manner in which you quilt. Insufficient basting will cause the layers to shift, creating tucks and irregularities in the backing as you quilt. Align all corners, pin in place, and using a contrasting thread, take long basting stitches that can easily be removed later. Start in the center and work out, as shown in Basting Diagram.

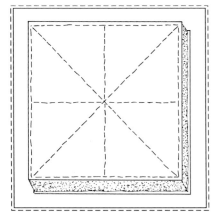

Basting Diagram

QUILTING

The actual quilting process is the connection of the three layers with tiny stitches. Many quilters find quilting the most rewarding and relaxing time spent with their project. Whether it is by hand or by machine, the quilting adds an all-important third dimension to your work by creating subtle shadows and nuances of depth that highlight the piecework. Two distinct forms of quilting, hand quilting and machine quilting, serve varying needs and accommodate a multitude of quilting requirements. Only by trial and error can you discover the technique best suited to you.

Hand Quilting

Hand quilting can refer to all of these: freehand stitching without a hoop or frame; hand stitching within a portable hoop or frame that permits turning the item being stitched for easy access; or hand stitching on a quilt that is attached to a large, standing quilting frame. Each of these hand-quilting methods has its own peculiarities; however, certain basic needle-and-thread techniques apply.

Hand quilting with or without a frame or hoop requires a running stitch. The needle enters the layers at an angle, while the fingers of the off hand ensure that all three layers are caught in each stitch. (I would encourage you to use a thimble or something to protect the middle finger of your off hand that is acting as a guide underneath the block). In this method of quilting, the bottom stitches can become slightly displaced. Do not pull the thread too tight.

When you are working with a supported hoop, I suggest using the rocking method of quilting. With the needle point aimed toward you, steer the eye of the needle with the tip of the thimble. (An indented thimble is ideal for the job.) The thumb is out in front to balance the up-and-down rocking motion, while underneath, the other hand works to help free the material. This method produces bottom stitches that line up with the top stitches in a consistent manner. Using a supported hoop allows you to turn your work around, offering easy accessibility to all sides without the hoop rim resting inside your elbows.

With the traditional standing frame, you quilt in two directions (unless you are ambidextrous) with a similar rocking motion. This takes some preplanning. Dangling threads that can be picked up to quilt in the opposite direction work well here, since it is most difficult to quilt while standing on one's head! Moving to the opposite side of the frame is an alternative way to get a new quilting angle. With a frame, the tension of the material is maintained by adjusting the screw on the side.

Now for the quilting: Naturally we all take pride in our small, consistent stitches, but that one uneven stitch in a row of otherwise perfect stitches imparts the warmth of the human touch. Take small, consistently uneven stitches (a sewing machine would make consistently even stitches), about 6 to 10 per inch. Let your off hand gently hold the material and check to see that the needle point has come through all 3 layers. Also use your off hand to be sure there is no overlapping of backing material. If overlapping occurs, stop, take the offending quilting stitches out, and start again. Try to take up the same amount of material on the top and the backing.

Whether or not you use a frame, always start your quilting in the center of the basted block to prevent the fabric from puckering. Then proceed to the outside edges. Quilt right angle lines first, and then go on to the diagonal lines where the fabric has more give. Remember to stop quilting ½" to 1" short of the outside edge of your block so that you can connect the blocks later. Try to put approximately the same amount of quilting in each block; your stitches will take up some of the fabric, but you want the blocks to be the same size. This is especially important in sampler quilts.

With all forms of quilting, a hidden knot is essential, and the fewer knots, the more durable the quilt. When possible, sneak the needle through the batting to the next area to be quilted rather than ending off with a knot. A thread that is cut too long and pulled through the layers repeatedly will wear and fray. The use of beeswax is optional; quilting thread comes with a coating. You can eliminate a knot when starting by using a double length of quilting thread, about 30" long. Pull only 15" of the thread through; quilt that length out, and then return to the 15" that was left dangling and quilt that out. When you reach the ends of the thread, form a knot by making a loop with the thread. Use the point of the needle to keep the knot close to the fabric as the thread is pulled tight. Take a half backstitch, bringing up the needle about an inch away. Tug the knot through the front, leaving the knot hidden in the layer of batting. Clip the dangling thread end. (Sometimes a dangling thread is left on the outside edge of the block, to be picked up and used for quilting after the blocks are assembled.)

The foolproof knot: This knot is used when you prefer to begin quilting with a knotted thread, and you want to hide the knot in the batting before taking any stitches. To make a foolproof knot, thread the needle with 12" to 18" of thread. Draw the thread into a circle and hold with the eye of the needle between your right thumb and forefinger. (See Foolproof Knot Diagram I.)

Wrap the thread around the

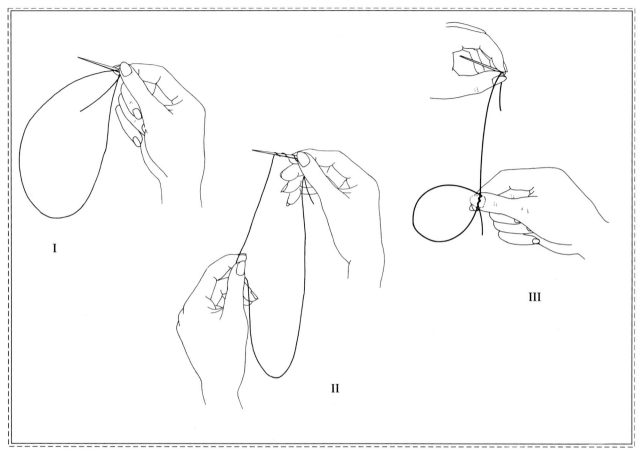

Foolproof Knot Diagrams

needle 2 or 3 times with your left hand. Slide this coil of thread down the needle until you can hold it, along with the eye and the thread end, in your right hand. (See Foolproof Knot Diagram II.) Holding the tip of the needle with your left hand, slide the coil down the thread until it tightens. (See Foolproof Knot Diagram III.) Trim any tail off the end. After a little practice, you will have a perfect knot every time.

For open, loosely woven fabric, try wrapping the thread around the needle 3 or 4 times. For tightly woven fabric, just 1 or 2 wraps will do.

Machine Quilting

Please don't be afraid to try machine quilting. Our machine piecework today has allowed us to create a mountain of quilt tops that are just waiting to be quilted. Machine quilting with a strong lock stitch saves us time and allows us to quilt more quilts. When you think about it—won't we stay just as warm under a machine-quilted quilt? Of course!

Machine quilting a full-size, layered quilt is very difficult because of the amount of fabric you must handle. Machine quilting in sections is a logical solution to the problem. These sections can be blocks or rows, but remember to leave ½" free at outside connecting edges. This is just as important as in hand quilting. When machine quilting, never try to emulate hand quilting; instead, take advantage of your sewing machine's capabilities.

Basting is just as important for machine work as for hand quilting, but be careful not to catch your basting stitches in the presser foot.

When you select your thread color, remember that the top thread and the bobbin thread can be the same color, or the bobbin thread can match the color of the backing. Never use quilting thread in the machine; it will not work. You might consider a monofilament thread or a variegated thread.

A zipper foot allows you to confine the machine stitching to the seams of the piecework; this technique, known as quilting in-the-ditch, is a very effective approach to quilting if you do not want stitching lines to spoil the look of your piecework.

Another form of machine quilting is done with a wide zigzag stitch sewn directly on top of the pieced seam, either through all 3 layers or just through the top and batting.

Using a hoop for machine quilting is optional. A thin hoop does stabilize the work; keep the larger hoop on the bottom and insert the smaller hoop on the top of the fabric. If you are quilting with the feed dogs up, the hoop must be moved as you progress. If the feed dogs are dropped, I find the hoop a necessity. This freewheeling form of quilting on the machine is sometimes called "loitering," "meandering," or "free motion."

Machine quilting like this does take concentration and some practice, but there is a flow of energy that rushes from mind to needle that is most exciting! Another machine-quilting technique called "thread sketching" calls for a particular design to be filled in with continuous straight or zigzag stitches. (I've found that my best machine quilting is done in the morning rather than after a full day's work.) ◆

NOW, ASSEMBLE THE QUILT

After many enjoyable hours of quilting, the assembly of your quilt can begin. Clean up the blocks by removing all the basting threads, masking tape, and any fabric marker lines. Trim all sides of the blocks so that the block, batting, and backing are even. The key to successful lap quilting is uniformity of block size. Working on a clean floor or a bed, arrange the blocks and establish rows that can be connected, either horizontally or vertically. If you've sketched the overall design for your quilt, you already have the map you need to put your blocks together. If not, you will want to play with your blocks until you achieve a good balance of color and design. If your quilt is a sampler, alternate four-patch and nine-patch blocks.

Once you have all of your blocks laid out, take a few steps back, squint your eyes, and be sure that you like what you see. Mark each block with a fabric marker or make a simple diagram on paper so that you will remember the final setting.

You'll first assemble the horizontal rows and then attach the rows to each other. This process is the same for Method A (bordered) or Method B (4-block) arrangements.

BLOCK-TO-BLOCK ASSEMBLY

In block-to-block assembly, the blocks are first assembled in horizontal rows. The tops of the blocks are machine-sewn to one another, leaving the backing free to be hand-sewn in a flat, lapped seam.

1. Select 2 adjacent blocks and stack them on a flat surface with right sides facing. Pin the backing and batting away from the seam to be sewn, revealing the raw edges of the front of the block. (See Block-to-Block Assembly Diagram I.)
2. Pin the fronts of 2 blocks together at the corners and in the center, easing where necessary. Machine-stitch, leaving a ¼" seam allowance. You may release 1 side of the batting and include it in the

seam at this time, but remember to keep the batting against the feed dogs to prevent it from being caught in the needle. (Block-to-Block

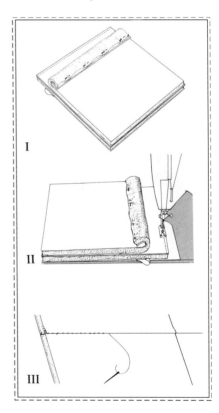

Block-To-Block Assembly Diagrams

Assembly Diagram II.)

3. Continue to sew the blocks together in this way until the row is complete. Thumb-crease the seams closed and all in one direction. Alternate the direction of the creased seam from one row to the next.

4. Lay the row of assembled blocks with the backing side up. Unpin the backing and batting. Trim the batting in the attached blocks so that it butts up against the adjacent batting but does not overlap it.

5. Smooth the backing of one of the blocks over the seam and batting. Turn under the other backing ¼" and slipstitch this flat lapped seam in place with coordinating thread, taking care not to go through to the top of the block. (See Block-to-Block Assembly Diagram III.)

If keeping your quilting stitches away from the edges of your blocks prevented you from putting in all the quilting you wanted, you can quilt close to the edges after the blocks are assembled with the aid of a quilting hoop. Or, you can quilt along the edges before the folded lap of backing is stitched into place. This second method is particularly

useful when working with mitered corners.

This entire block-to-block assembly process can be reversed. The backings may be machine-stitched together and the seams on the front of the quilt slipstitched in place.

ROW-TO-ROW ASSEMBLY

Once the blocks are connected in rows, you can begin the row-to-row assembly. This will take a lot of space, so you may want to set up your machine on a large surface such as a dining room table. Consult your diagrams for the correct order in which the rows are to be connected. If at some point during this next step you become discouraged, just remember, the quilting is all done and this is the last leg of the journey. Two methods of row-to-row assembly are described here. The method you choose depends on your batting thickness and on how the outside edges of the quilt are to be treated.

Method 1

This method works best when using thick batting or when a ruffle,

border, or extra edging is to be added later. It is exactly the same as block-to-block assembly. Pin the backing and unattached batting of the assembled blocks away from the fronts. Align the intersections of the rows and secure with pins. (Basting will help to ease fabric between intersections.) Machine-stitch the rows together with a ¼" seam. (See Row-to-Row Assembly

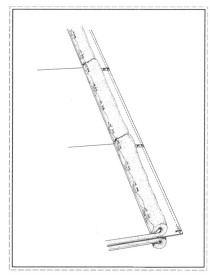

Row-To-Row Assembly Diagram I

Diagram I.) If using a medium-weight batting and bias edging, one side of the batting could be released and included in the seam. (See

Row-to-Row Assembly Diagram II.)
Backstitch at each end of the row.

Spread out the connected rows

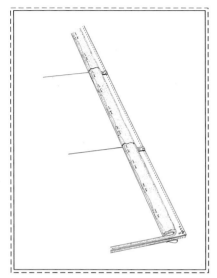

Row-To-Row Assembly Diagram II

on a large flat surface with the backing side up. Crease each row's seam in the same direction. Trim the batting, so it just butts together. Smooth the backing of one row over the seam and batting. Turn under the backing of the other row ¼", pin or baste, and slipstitch by hand. Be careful not to take stitches through the quilt top during this step. (See Row-to-Row Assembly Diagram III.)

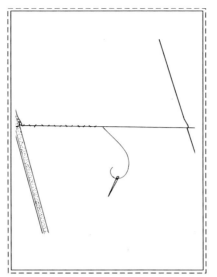

Row-To-Row Assembly Diagram III

Method 2

If you are using a lightweight batting, you can choose to connect 5 layers, as opposed to 2 or 3 layers as described in Method 1. Baste these 5 layers (backing, batting, top, top, batting), carefully aligning the intersections of your rows. Machine-stitch the 5 layers together, as shown in Row-to-Row Assembly Diagram IV. Turn the only remaining layer, the unattached backing, under ¼" and slipstitch in place.

If after your whole quilt is assembled, you find areas that you wanted to quilt before, see

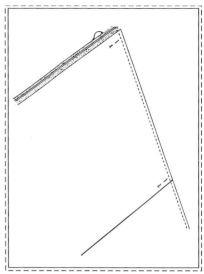

Row-To-Row Assembly Diagram IV

Block-to-Block Assembly.

BORDERS

Even if you have already quilted your quilt, you can add pieced or plain bands to enlarge it or frame it. Any band or pieced border that is added has to be cut the length of the side before quilting, as there is a certain amount of "take-up" due to quilting. After the border addition is attached, quilting needs to be added for balance. The borders need to work with the design of the entire unit.

The "stack" method is a quick and easy way to attach this addition. With raw edges aligned, stack in the following manner: backing of border, right side up; the quilt top, right side up; border top, wrong side up; and finally, border batting, as shown in Stack and Extend Diagram. Baste and machine-stitch these layers together with the batting next to the machine feed dogs. Fold layers outward, baste, and quilt. This process is sometimes called "stack and extend." If all the strips or bands are cut the same width, this is a quick way of making a quilt, because the front and back are made at the same time. ◆

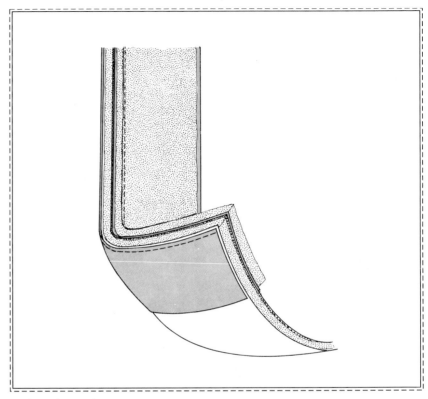

Stack And Extend Diagram

A quilt isn't complete until you add a proper finished edge. There are several considerations at this point. Is the quilt the right size? Will the quilt rest on a larger-sized bed than you had originally intended, and therefore, need a border? Do you want a novelty addition of ruffles or lace? Consider the style of the quilt. For instance, neither curved piecework nor appliqué lends itself to sharp triangular accents. A key to a successful finish is planning. Plan your finishing touches as carefully as you planned the rest of your quilt.

BINDINGS AND EDGES

Have you ever wondered why a double-fold bias edge is preferable to a straight-of-the-grain edging for your quilt? It's because the outside edge of a quilt gets a lot of wear and is often the first thing to deteriorate. One thread resting at the edge in a straight-of-the-grain fabric receives so much wear that it will soon fray with use, but diagonal threads from a bias can distribute the wear and tear. A double-fold bias offers even more protection.

Bias binding may be purchased, or you can make your own. Making your own is more economical and allows you to coordinate the binding with the quilt. But sometimes it's hard to figure how much fabric to buy for a continuous bias strip for a finished quilt or pillow ruffle. If you know how wide a bias edging you want and the length or the measurement of the perimeter of your quilt, the chart below will help you to determine the amount of fabric you need for the quilts. It may also be helpful when you're doing other home decorating projects.

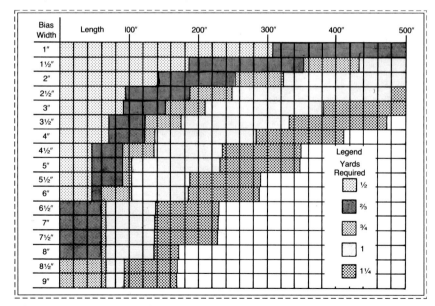

Chart For Determining Yardage Required for Making Bias Binding

Bias Binding

How to estimate bias length:

To determine the length of bias you need to make or purchase, first measure the perimeter of your quilt. The following table will help.

METHOD A	
Baby quilt size	5 yards
Afghan size	7 yards
Twin size	8 yards
Double size	9 yards
Queen size	11 yards
King size	13 yards
METHOD B	
Baby quilt size	5¼ yards
Afghan size	6¾ yards
Twin size	9¼ yards
Double size	10½ yards
King size	13¼ yards

Making a Continuous Bias

Strip: Start with a square piece of fabric. Eliminate the selvage and cut the fabric in half on the diagonal to form two equal triangles. (See Bias Strip Diagram I.) Lay the two triangles, right sides together, so that right angles are at top, as shown in Bias Strip Diagram II. Machine-stitch with a ¼" seam allowance. Press seam open. Now the triangles will form a parallelogram. (See Bias Strip Diagram III.) Decide how wide you want the bias strip; 2½" to 3" is usually appropriate for the outside of a quilt. Mark this measurement with a pencil or fabric marker. (Your finished binding will actually be one-fourth the width of the bias strip.) Make a 6"-long cut down the line you have just marked. Continue to mark (but don't cut) across the entire parallelogram to make a guide for cutting. A see-through ruler helps with this step.

Join the right sides of A and B together so that points x and o meet. Sew with a ¼" seam allowance, joining side A to side B to form a tube. (See Bias Strip Diagram IV.) Notice that the 6"-long cut extends beyond the side of the tube, and the other side has about the same amount of excess. Use the loose 6" strip as a starting point to continue cutting the strip around the tube. Keep folding it back, being careful not to cut the fabric underneath.

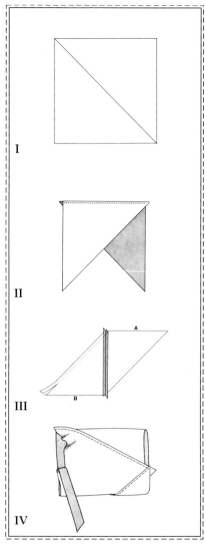

Bias Strip Diagrams

Attaching a Continuous Bias Strip: Hand-baste the outside edges of the quilt together to eliminate any pull of fabric. Straight pins placed at a right angle every inch or so will help to eliminate any pull, but basting is foolproof. Fold the continuous bias strip in half, aligning raw edges. Press. Starting at the midpoint on one side of the quilt (not in a corner), pin or baste the strip to the quilt with the strip's fold toward the inside and its raw edges aligned with the raw edges of the quilt. Where the ends of the bias strip meet, allow 4" of the strip to overlap. Machine-stitch the strip to the quilt with a ¼" seam allowance. Leave the overlapping 4" of the strip unstitched.

To join the ends of the strip unfold the left extension (unstitched section) and align the top raw edge with the raw edge of the quilt. Then unfold the right extension and overlap the left extension. Mark an X on the endpoint of the right extension and on the left extension where it meets the right. On the left extension, mark ½" to the right of the X. (See Attaching Bias Binding Diagram.)

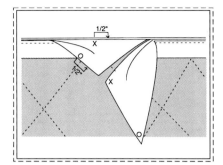

Attaching Bias Binding Diagram

Then reverse the procedure. Place the right extension against the quilt top, and overlap it with the left extension. Mark an O on the right side of each extension where they meet. On the right side of the left extension, mark ½" to the right of the O. Draw a diagonal line connecting the second set of marks on the left extension. Then cut on this line, as shown in Attaching Bias Binding Diagram.

Sew the ends of the extensions together with a ¼" seam allowance. Fold the bias strip and finish sewing it to the quilt. Then roll the strip over the raw edges and slipstitch it in place on the back of the quilt just over the machine stitching.

A perfectly squared-off corner requires a right angle to be formed with a double bias edging. To do this, use a fabric marker and mark the inside ¼" turn at each corner of the quilt. Sew the bias strip up to that mark and backstitch, as shown in Squared-Off Corner Diagram I. Remove your work from the machine.

Turn the raw edge of the bias strip at the corner of the quilt and make a ½" fold. Pinch or pin this together. (See Squared-Off Corner Diagram II.)

Align the raw edges and machine-stitch perpendicular to the

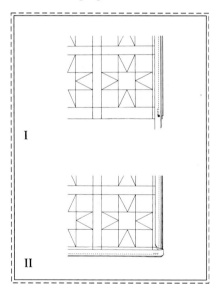

Squared-Off Corner Diagrams

previous backstitching. This will create a perfect diagonal fold on the front and back when the bias strip is folded over. Continue attaching the bias strip to all the raw edges of the quilt.

Once you have machine-sewn the bias strip to the quilt top, roll the bias strip over the raw edges and slipstitch in place on the back of the quilt just beyond the machine stitching. This must be done by hand.

Rolled Hems

A rolled hem can be used on the front or back of a quilt if each of the perimeter blocks is cut with a 1" extension on the outside edge. Simply fold the extension to the opposite side of the quilt, turn under ¼", and then secure it with a slipstitch.

Self-Finished Edges

Self-finished edges are possible only if the outside edges of the quilt are free of quilting. Trim the batting about ¼" and turn the raw edges of both the front and back in toward each other. Pin in place and secure with a running stitch. This produces square corners and a nice

neat finish to the quilt edge.

Ruffles or Lace

Consider adding a gathered ruffle, eyelet, or even a double ruffle to the border of your quilt. To do this, pin the loose backing away from the batting and front of the quilt. Baste or pin the ruffle or accent to the batting and the front. Machine-sew ¼" beyond any gathering line. Always have the batting next to the feed dogs and not next to the machine needle. Trim any excess seam allowance; fold seam allowance toward the quilt. Turn backing under ¼" and slipstitch in place over the line of machine stitching. A deep ruffle added to your quilt might be an alternative to a separate dust ruffle on your bed.

Sawtooth Edge

Folded triangles intermesh into a sawtooth design (often called prairie points) for a clever accent to many quilt designs. Any size of square may be used to form your triangles. (Five-inch squares folded into triangles fit nicely into an 18" border span.) Fold the squares in half into triangles and then fold again to

form smaller triangles. Interlap the triangles around the perimeter of the quilt, as shown in Sawtooth Edge Diagram. Pin or baste in place and attach as you would a ruffle. Small triangle accents are nice on a baby quilt.

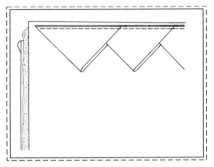

Sawtooth Edge Diagram

Scalloped Edges

For a scalloped edging, sew two circles of material together around edges. Cut through the diameter and turn right side out to form two half circles. Sew the half circles side by side to form a lovely scalloped edge.

If you like the look of a scalloped edge, but would prefer to be able to quilt it, it is best to sew a three-layered edging before attaching it to the quilt. In this case, make each quilt side's edging out of pieces of continuous fabric. Make a template and trace the scallop design onto the wrong side of your quilt top fabric with the straight edge on the straight of the grain. Stack this piece of fabric with pieces of batting and backing the same size; stack batting, backing fabric right side up, and then quilt top fabric wrong side up. Baste the three layers together and then machine-stitch along the curved edge of the scalloped border, taking an extra horizontal stitch at each "V" before sewing around the next curve. (See Scalloped Edge Diagram.) Trim all three layers along the straight edge of the scallop and around the now-sewn curves; turn inside out and attach to the raw edges of the quilt.

This same method can be used to attach a scalloped border to an

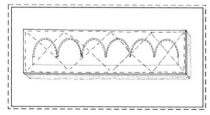

Scalloped Edge Diagram

already edged quilt. Quilting can be done on the scalloped edge or

border after attaching it to the quilt.

Another version of the scalloped edge can be made by actually cutting scallops into the perimeters of the blocks that will form the outside edges of the quilt. This method calls for tracing the scallop design on the wrong side of the appropriate edge of the block before it is quilted. Baste block backing and batting together and put the right sides of the block and backing together so that machine stitching of the three layers is possible, following the curved scallop. Here again, take one horizontal stitch at the "V" between curves to give a flat, easy turn. Trim away excess material; turn right side out, and baste. Quilt close to the perimeter edge.

Once the bias strip is made, fold it in half with raw edges aligned and gently press. Place the folded bias strip on top of the quilt with the fold toward the inside, and pin in place or baste. Machine-stitch the entire folded bias strip to the quilt top with a ¼" seam allowance. Corners may be rounded off by gently curving the bias strip at each turn.

THE SIGNATURE

Finding a quilt that is personal and appealing is a treat. Discovering a date and initials on it is truly exciting. So take the time to add that final touch for posterity on your own quilt. Either by hand or machine, sign and date your quilt in one corner. This completes the story and highlights all the many steps—and the love—involved in making a quilt.

If there is a personal dedication that you want to display, type the message directly on a piece of muslin. Prepare a cloth frame and insert this muslin fabric inside. Now, stand back and call all your friends to join in this glorious moment of completion. ◆

INDEX